How your child's LeapReader works

Helps children build **reading**, **writing,** and **listening skills** with an interactive book reader and audio player. LeapReader is designed to enhance vocabulary development and reading comprehension to help children become confident, independent readers and writers.

LeapReader modes

Audio Books   Music   Trivia Fun

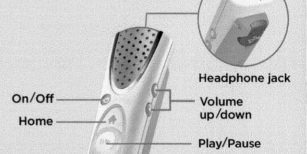

Headphone jack

On/Off

Home

Volume up/down

Play/Pause

Forward/Back

 Read the Page

  Game

 Repeat

 Read the Story

Lvl 1   Lvl 2   Lvl 3

 Stop

boy girl

Aa Bb Cc Dd Ee Ff Gg

Hh Ii Jj Kk Ll Mm

Nn Oo Pp Qq Rr Ss Tt

Uu Vv Ww Xx Yy Zz

Ozzie and Mack

written by Trish Holland

illustrated by Dan Krall

 Ozzie Otter broke a rule
when he brought his pet to school.
In the pack on Ozzie's back,
sat a little bug named Mack.

"Not one sound. Do not forget,"
Ozzie said to Mack, his pet.
"You'll go home if Teacher sees.
Stay inside and don't move, please."

But that speedy bug jumped out onto Foster Fox's snout.

Foster whispered, "Catch him quick or I think I may be sick."

Ozzie reached, but Mack hopped over
onto Sylvie Squirrel's shoulder.

Sylvie said, "Your bug is here,
hiding right behind my ear."

Mrs. Bunny turned around.
"No more noise. Please, sit back down.
Time to sing our A-B-Cs,
then we'll count our 1-2-3s."

Ozzie, Foster, Sylvie, too,
did not know quite what to do,
so they sang out loud and strong.
On the floor, Mack danced along.

Ozzie tried a tackle then.

Mack just bounced away again.

Next he leaped up on a shelf.

Mack would not behave himself!

Mack turned cartwheels way up high.

"This is trouble," Ozzie sighed.

Mack flew out across the room.
Then there came a great, big—

Papers fluttered in the air.
Books and pages everywhere.

"EEEEK!" shrieked Teacher.
"What is that?"

Mack is who she pointed at.

"This is Mack.
He loves to play.
He'll be good.
Please let him stay."

Teacher said, "You know the rule."
"You may not bring pets to school!"
A plan was needed, Ozzie knew.
Watching Mack, he found a clue.

"I can read this book to you.
That is something I can do."

Students listened like they should.
Teacher saw Mack could be good.
Mrs. Bunny scratched her head,
tapped her foot, and then she said,

"I will change that silly rule.
You may all bring pets to school."

Ozzie Otter shouted, "Yay!
Teacher says that Mack can stay!"

In the morning, pets came, too.
How the story circle grew!

On the top of Teacher's head
sat a little bug named Ned.

All the students laughed out loud.
Mrs. Bunny beamed, so proud.

dog
fog
bog
hog
log
frog

Ozzie's Rhyme Time Band

mug bug
jug slug
plug rug

cat
hat
bat
rat
mat

21

cub

bit

mad

kit

tap

not

pet

rip

Tree House Telephone

note

made

Pete

ripe

kite

e

bite

cube

tape

River Roundup

dock

picnic

snorkel

canoe

paddle

nest

hive

school of fish

waterfall

dive